I0617852

Peace, Sex, and Sensuality

Introduce Your Inner Goddess to Your Everyday Life On This
Eight Week Journey to Wholeness.

by

Latoya Jones

ISBN-978-1-960853-26-4

Liberation's Publishing LLC
West Point - Mississippi

Peace, Sex,
and Sensuality

Introduce Your Inner Goddess to Your Everyday Life On This
Eight Week Journey to Wholeness.

Table of Contents

"The most important relationship in your life is the one you have with yourself."

-Diane Von Furstenberg

❀ Self-Evaluation

Welcome Goddess, I am so excited to get started on this amazing journey with you! My desire for you is by the end of this eight-week workbook, you will experience a shift in your mindset and how you view the world around you. The world around us can make us view ourselves, *bodies, sexuality, and lives,* in a poor or negative light. This self-evaluation will help you see where you stand now. After the eight-weeks, you will take another self-evaluation to see how much your mindset has changed. Please fill out and answer the questions listed below. Remember, there are no right or wrong answers just honest ones!

On a scale from 1 to 10, with one being the lowest (extremely poor) to ten being the highest (excellent), please answer the following questions. Note: Some questions may ask you to explain your answer.

1. What level would you rate your self-confidence?

    a. 1 2 3 4 5 6 7 8 9 10

    b. What would help increase your self-confidence?

    c. _____

    _____

    _____

    _____

2. What level would you rate your self-care routine?

    a. 1 2 3 4 5 6 7 8 9 10

3. What level would you rate your sex life?

    a. 1 2 3 4 5 6 7 8 9 10

4. What level would you rate your love life?

    a. 1 2 3 4 5 6 7 8 9 10

5. Overall, what level would you rate your happiness?

    a. 1 2 3 4 5 6 7 8 9 10

    b. Please explain why you chose this rating for your overall happiness.

    c. _____

    _____

    _____

    _____

6. How well can you communicate your desires and wants to your partner or anyone else in your life?

    a. 1 2 3 4 5 6 7 8 9 10

    b. Is there anyone you can NOT express desires and wants to at all? Yes or No

    c. Please explain why.

    d. _____

    _____

    _____

    _____

Please answer yes or no to the following questions:

1. Do you feel comfortable with your body? Yes or No
2. Do you feel you are normal when it comes to sex? Yes or No
3. Do you often compare yourself in a negative way to models or other women? Yes or No
4. Do you find it difficult to stay on track when it comes to taking care of yourself? Yes or No
5. Parents or Caregivers Only: Do you find it difficult to feel and or look sexy while being a parent or caregiver? Yes or No

Please answer the following questions:

1. What are you experiencing right now that you do not want to experience?
   a. _____
      _____
      _____

2. How do you want to feel on a daily basis?
   a. _____
      _____
      _____

3. What would you like to happen to you?
   a. _____
      _____
      _____

Peace, Sex, *and Sensuality*

.

❀Week One

This first week may be the most emotionally challenging week. When I say opening yourself up to yourself, I mean just that! This week we will dive deep into our fears, discouragements, and negative narratives. This is the weed pulling week. It may not be the most fun task, but it is a necessary one. By completing this we can start to have a full, lush, and beautiful emotional garden.

Day 1 Exercise 1: Deep Rooted Fears

Please use the space below to write down three deep rooted fears and explain why these are your fears. Remember, there are no wrong answers, just honest ones.

Example 1: *I am afraid to have sex with the lights on because I am deeply ashamed of my body. I am ashamed and disgusted with my body and I am afraid my lover will be too.*

Example 2: *I am afraid to speak up or defend myself verbally anywhere. I was always told to "shut up" and no one cares about how I feel. I don't want to feel powerless or ignored.*

1. _____
   _____
   _____

2. _____
   _____
   _____

3. _____
   _____
   _____

Please write in the space below how these fears are negatively impacting your life.

Example 1: *My fear of my lover hating my body causes stress on our sex life. I avoid all conversations that may lead to us talking about sex. This is starting to make my lover frustrated. They are beginning to think they are the problem.*

Example 2: *Not speaking up has made me miss possible promotions and is keeping me stuck in an unsatisfying romantic relationship. Not speaking up about my feelings is holding me back from the life I really want.*

1. _____
   _____
   _____

2. _____
   _____
   _____

3. _____
   _____
   _____

Day 1 Exercise 2: Rewrite Your Outcome

Our minds create fear in a way to protect us from possible dangerous outcomes. Fear is there to help keep us safe and alive. For example, the fear of going down a dark alley by yourself. Therefore, fear in some cases can be a good thing. However, in most cases like our day to day lives, certain fears can stop us from obtaining the life that we really desire. In this exercise I want you to rewrite your fears. In addition, write down two positive outcomes if you move forward in spite of those fears. Leave two positive outcomes for each fear.

Facing fears can open up a world of beautiful possibilities.

1. _____
   _____
   _____

2. _____
   _____
   _____

3. _____
   _____
   _____

After seeing some possible positive outcomes attached to your fears, are you willing to face one of them or maybe all three of them? Yes or No

Why or Why not?

_____
_____
_____

Day 1 Self-Care Exercise: Breathe

Breathing is so important and yet we do not take the time to do it. This breathing exercise is designed to help you relieve stress. You can also use breathing exercises before you choose to face one of your fears. Note: If you feel like you're going to pass out please do not continue to hold your breath.

This breathing exercise can be done anywhere and anytime you feel a little anxious. You can do this four times if you need to.

- ❀ Sit up straight and make yourself comfortable.
- ❀ Close your eyes.
- ❀ Breathe in for 4 seconds.
- ❀ Hold your breath for 4 seconds.
- ❀ Breathe out for 4 seconds.
- ❀ Repeat

Journaling: Throughout the rest of this course, we ae going to practice journaling our thoughts every day. Journaling is a great exercise that can help you relieve stress, inspire creativity, boost your memory, and allow you to self-reflect. For Day 1 take a moment to reflect on your day and how these exercises did or did not help you. If not reflect on why it didn't.

Planning: Throughout the rest of this course, we will practice using a planner. We believe that we don't have enough time when in fact it is due to lack of proper planning. Sometimes we waste time doing things that are not important, urgent or things we can delegate to others. Planning will help you see how much time you have and help you prioritize.

For the rest of week one, plan an hour for yourself and for the end of the week (weekend if you prefer) plan two hours for yourself. Note: The hour doesn't have to be consecutive. For example, taking 15-minute breaks throughout your day to participate in a breathing exercise, walking or even just sitting and listening to music is perfectly fine.

Plan 15-20 minutes for Day 2 Exercises!

Day 2 Exercise 1

Write down what you do not like about your body and why. For example: *I don't like my thighs because you can see the cellulite when I walk.* You can only write up to five things that you do not like about your body. If you have less than five, wonderful!

1. _____
2. _____
3. _____
4. _____
5. _____

Journaling: Write down any additional thoughts that you have about the body parts above. For example: if you are comparing your body to what you used to look like before you had children or before you became an adult. Write down as little or as much as you'd like.

Day 2 Exercise 2

You will need a full-length mirror, lipstick, and privacy. For this exercise you will need to strip down to your bra and panties in front of your mirror. For some Goddesses this may be a difficult task. Please be patient and kind to yourself. Acknowledge any feelings that may bubble up.

With the lipstick, you are going to draw a heart on the five places you do not like. While drawing the heart, you are going to thank the body part for doing something wonderful for you! For example: "Thank you belly for carrying my children, for digesting delicious food, and for doing a wonderful job at being my torso!"

Make sure that you use lipstick that is easy to remove when you shower.

Day 2 Self-Care Exercise: Breathe

  ❋   Sit up straight and make yourself comfortable.

- Close your eyes.
- Breathe in for 4 seconds.
- Hold your breath for 4 seconds.
- Breathe out for 4 seconds.
- Repeat

Journaling: After you are all cleaned up and relaxed, write down how you feel about your body part now. Do you feel a little different? Do you feel the same? What needs to happen for you to like or love this particular body part?

Planning: Do you have any important meetings coming up? Anything that you feel anxious about? If so, plan an extra 5 or 10 minutes to breathe and relax before the scheduled tasks.

Day 3 Exercise 1

We all have strengths and weaknesses. These are not deeply rooted fears that stop us from achieving our goals, these are minor annoyances that may slow us down. We all have strengths and weaknesses. The goal is to recognize your weaknesses and strengths.

Write down five weaknesses and how having these weaknesses slow you down from obtaining your goal. For example, "I have poor self-talk." This really slows me down from trying something different or new, because I have convinced myself that I can't do it."

1. _____
   _____
   _____

2. _____
   _____
   _____

3. _____
   _____
   _____

4. _____
   _____
   _____

5. _____
   _____
   _____

Day 3 Exercise 2

Our strengths can be easily overlooked sometimes. We often don't see the good in ourselves as easily as we see it in others. In this exercise write down five strengths that you have and how they benefit your life. For example: "I can communicate my feelings very well. The benefit that this brings to my life is understanding. The people that I love and care for understand me a little bit better."

1. _____
   _____
   _____

2. _____
   _____
   _____

3. _____
   _____
   _____

4. _____
   _____
   _____

5. _____
   _____
   _____

Day 3 Self-Care Exercise: Breathe

This breathing technique can also be used to help calm your body down after a stressful situation.

- Find a comfortable seated position or lie down.
- Breathe slowly for 5 seconds.
- Hold your breath for 1 second.
- Breathe out slowly for 7 seconds.

Journaling: for this journal entry, write down how you can turn your weaknesses into strengths. Think about what small daily goals you can set to help improve on your weaknesses. For example, "I am a poor communicator. I will watch at least one video a week about communication and try to participate in the future business meetings."

It is important to acknowledge any feelings that may come up while you are writing your small daily goals. If it's fear or anxiety do one of the breathing exercises and write down those fears and anxieties.

Planning: Practice makes progress. It is important to practice the daily goals you have set. In your planner, set some time aside to practice turning your weakness into a strength. If you can't do them daily, make sure that you are being as consistent as possible.

Day 4 Exercise 1

Journaling: This is the exercise where you will need some time to dive deep into your beliefs. You will need to write down your negative beliefs in your journal. Along with writing down the negative beliefs, you also must write down where those beliefs came from. Understanding your negative mindset and where it started will help you rewrite a more positive forward-thinking story.

Acknowledge any feelings that come up. Write those feelings down. Take breaks if you need to and practice the self-care breathing exercises. Cry if you feel that is necessary. These negative beliefs can be deeply tied to your womanhood, race, spirituality, body, etc. so in short, these beliefs are very personal to you. When breaking these beliefs, you are breaking the emotional attachment that comes along with them.

Day 4 Self-Care Exercise: Breathe

This breathing technique can also be used to help calm your body down after a stressful situation.

- Find a comfortable seated position or lie down.
- Breathe slowly for 5 seconds.
- Hold your breath for 1 second.
- Breathe out slowly for 7 seconds.

Planning: Schedule some time for reflecting for Day five and six. This time can be added into your bedtime routine with a cup of hot tea if you desire. Day seven prepare for week two.

Reflection days are just as important as activity days. These days are added to allow you time to reflect on yourself without exercises. It is important to journal during these days.

Congratulations Goddess!

You've just completed Week 1 of introducing your inner goddess to your everyday life!

❀Week Two

Treat Yourself Like a Goddess!

Now that we have dumped some negative views about ourselves and our bodies, let's start refilling ourselves with some kindness. Yup, you guessed it, this is week two of the "Peace" part of the program. This is the kindness part. This is the self-love part.

Day 1 Exercise 1: An ode to your body and mind! Yes, that is right, you are going to write a poem that is fit for a Goddess. You are to write the most beautiful poem about yourself. Add wonderful loving adjectives about your parts, your loving bits! Write it as if you are to impress a Goddess.

(Title of Poem)

Journaling: Write about the exercise today. How did it make you feel? Awkward? Was it outrageous to write wonderful things about yourself in this format? Why or why not. Allow yourself to dive deep with this journal entry. Week one only opened you up to yourself a little bit, there might be more layers that you have to work through.

Self-Care Exercise: Pick one of the two breathing exercises that you have learned last week. Yes, we are still breathing!

Planner: Schedule some time in the morning (before work) or during your morning routine to do Day 2 Exercise 1

Day 2 Exercise 1

For this exercise we are going to honor ourselves with a poem. Go back to the poem you wrote about your gorgeous self and read it out loud while standing in the mirror. Make sure you are reading it with meaning and passion. Do this twice.

After you have allowed those wonderful words to set in, evaluate yourself. For example, the first time I read the poem I giggled! I thought it was silly, but the second time I allowed the words to sink in. (Please be as detailed as possible)

Evaluation:_____

_____

_____

_____

_____

_____

_____

_____

_____

_____

_____

_____

_____

_____

_____

_____

_____

Day 2 Exercise 2: Affirmations. Go back to week 1 and look over your weaknesses. Find one weakness and create a positive affirmation from that weakness. For example, if you were a poor communicator you would say: "I am a brilliant communicator! I express my thoughts clearly and effortlessly!" Try to write 5 affirmations. (All 5 does not need to be created from your weaknesses).

1. _____

2. _____

3. _____

4. _____

5. _____

Journal: Write down your affirmations and acknowledge any feelings that bubble up. Did you feel awkward? Did you automatically reject the affirmation? Was the affirmation hard to believe? Explore these types of questions in your journal entry.

Self-Care Exercise: Sit in a comfortable position. Use one of the breathing exercises you have learned and imagine one of your affirmations already coming to past.

Planner: write down an affirmation you are going to repeat over the next five days. It might be helpful if you set a little reminder on your phone. *Pro Tip: Putting the affirmation as the alarm title on your phone can be a pleasant reminder in the middle of a tough day.

Day 3 Exercise 1

Writing the perfect workday. This exercise will help you imagine your perfect workday. Think about everything from the time you wake up until the time you go to bed. Design your perfect workday. Think about what you will wear, who you will work with, what you eat for lunch etc. *Be sure to include self-care activities.

Journaling: After acknowledging what would make your perfect day. Write about some obstacles you will have to overcome to make sure the day remains perfect. For example, if you have a coworker, you do not get along with or a project that you have yet to finish. Write how you might handle the situation if it arises. It is good to be proactive; this helps maintain your peace.

Self-Care: Find a gentle yoga video. Use their breathing techniques combined with the poses. The idea is to learn how to allow a bad day to move through you (allowing the stress response to come to completion) and allow a good day to radiate all through your body.

Planner: Make time for some gentle yoga this week. It is good to try new things.

Day 4 Exercise 1: Write your perfect day off. We often fantasize about the perfect day off; however, we leave it just a fantasize. We say we are going to book that massage but never do. We say we are going to learn that new language but never start. In this exercise, write down what will make your perfect day off beyond perfect!

Journal: We all have reasons why we keep ourselves from things that we love. In this journal entry, write down the reasons why you never allowed yourself to have your perfect day. Was it, kids and couldn't find a babysitter? Or was it money? Did bills always come first? While writing down the reasons why you didn't allow yourself to have the perfect day, acknowledge any feelings that bubble up.

Self-Care: Revisit the gentle yoga routine from the previous day.

Planner: Schedule some time for reflecting on Day 5 & 6. This time can be added to your bedtime routine with a cup of hot tea if you desire.

Reflection days are just as important as activity days. These days are added to the 8-week workbook to allow you time to reflect on your own without the exercises. It is important to journal during these days.

Congratulations Goddess,
You've Completed Week 2!

You've also completed the Peace part of the Goddess Workbook.

Peace is a huge part of our overall health. Finding peace within ourselves is the first step to living a more fulfilled life. It must be made clear, just because we completed the Peace part of our program, does not mean you stop reaching for it in your everyday life. Each Goddess must find the time for her to breathe and to gently move her beautiful body!

❀Week Three

Week 3 & 4 is working with Sex! Having a wonderful sex life does not come from having amazing sex with your partner, it is based off having amazing sex with! Yes, Goddess these next weeks are our exploration weeks.

Disclaimer: This may not be an easy journey for some Goddesses, but it is important to understand the level you are on.

Day 1 Exercise 1: Write down your favorite positions. Try to write down at least five different positions and the reasons why you enjoy these positions. For example: I love reverse cowgirl because it makes me feel naughty and in control. Write down three positions that you hate and the reasons why you hate them. For example: I don't like the missionary position, it seems a bit boring and outdated.

1. _____
   _____
   _____

2. _____
   _____
   _____

3. _____
   _____
   _____

4. _____
   _____
   _____

5. _____
   _____

Write 3 positions you hate and why:

1. _____
   _____
   _____

2. _____
   _____
   _____

3. _____
   _____
   _____

Journal: Knowing what we want as far as sexual positions is huge! However, communicating this during sex might not be the easiest task in the world. This journal entry, think about the yummy positions that you enjoy and the ones you despise. Imagine how you would make sure you get the yummy ones. Think about how you would communicate with your partner. Would you do it before sex? Would you do it during? As always, notice any feelings that may come up like anxiety or embarrassment. Acknowledge them.

Self-Care: Get to know her! Yes, this self-care exercise wants you to get to know your BFF (The Vagina) Your BFF is made up of so many different parts and has so many different sensations. This week we are just saying hello. Get a small mirror and have a look. Don't be shy, she is your best friend!

Planner: Make time to say hello to your BFF at least twice this week. Give her a few minutes of your time. It is very important to get to know her better.

Day 2 Exercise 1: Today we are going to explore toys. If you have a toy, great! You would just need to explore a new/different one. If you have never purchased one before, then this is your time to research them for yourself. The focus of this exercise is to expand your interests. I am not suggesting you purchase a toy but research some first. If you choose to purchase one because it sounds absolutely delicious to you…then awesome!

Before researching, let's write down what we want in pleasure. For example, I would like to have a toy that has both clitoral stimulation and penetration capabilities. Be open and honest with yourself. Do you want it to vibrate? No vibrate? Do you want it glass? Or realistic feel? After you have made your list research the toys that meet your requirements.

Pleasure Requirements:

1. _____
2. _____
3. _____
4. _____
5. _____
6. _____
7. _____
8. _____
9. _____
10._____

Found a toy you liked? If you want, you can write the name and information in the space below for safe keeping:

_____
_____
_____
_____

Journal: Today's exercise was to research a toy. Write about your experience. Did you actually go to an adult toy shop and explore/asked questions? Did you go online and browse through the many options the website might have had? Either way is absolutely fine! The point here is to write about how you felt about finding something new. Did you like the idea of possibly buying a toy? Do you feel that this toy will enhance your sex life or take away from it? Explore how you feel.

Self-Care: After a gorgeous bath or shower, give yourself an oil massage. Pay attention to your body and take your time. If you can do this self-care exercise in front of a mirror...PERFECT! If you get turned on while massaging yourself. That is perfectly fine too!

Planner: If you have a wax appointment, massage appointment, or anything of the sort that will make you feel sexy and you haven't booked it yet. Book it now! It doesn't have to be for the same week as week 3 but you must book something that makes you feel sexy!

Day 3 Exercise 1: Write the best sexual encounter you've experienced thus far. We are going to explore different elements of this particular encounter! Even if you were just pleasing you! When describing this wonderful experience include things like time of day, smells, were you stressed, how did you feel...etc. Try to be as detailed as possible.

Day 3 Exercise 2: For this exercise, you will need a highlighter of any color. In the previous exercise you were asked to describe your best sexual encounter. Use the highlighter to highlight some descriptive (adjectives) that you used. For example: I remembered the orgasms rippling through my body, it felt so delicious!

The purpose of this exercise is to understand your pleasure and how YOU view it! Notice the type of words you use or don't to describe your pleasure. This will help you communicate what you desire while in the moment. *Being able to communicate effectively about your pleasure and sexual desires takes practice and understanding yourself. So please be patient and kind to yourself.

After you highlight your adjective/descriptive words, list a few of your favorite ones below. If you want to describe your pleasure in a more colorful way, here is the place to do it Goddess!

1. _____

2. _____

3. _____

4. _____

5. _____

6. _____

7. _____

8. _____

9. _____

10. _____

Day 4 Exercise 1: There are many things we women do not understand about our bodies! Even our bodies when it comes to sexual responses have been studied with man in mind. Meaning, our vaginal responses, orgasms, arousal, etc. have been compared to a man's. Their sexual responses (through scientific studies) set the standard to OUR sexual responses. This is wrong. I don't need to tell you Goddess, but just in case, our bodies are a lot different than a man's body.

In this exercise think of a question or myth you believed about your sexual behavior, arousal, etc. as a woman and research it and write your findings below. This exercise will help you bust some beliefs that maybe holding you back from a very yummy sex life.

Question:

_____
_____
_____

What I found:

_____
_____
_____
_____

Journal: Write about things you did not know about your sexual self that you didn't discover until recently. It could be anything, from when you started this workbook to a book you've read that helps you understand your body better. Don't be afraid to keep asking questions, researching them, and write them down. Like always, take note on how you are feeling. For example, "What helped you find the courage to finally search for answers to a particular question pertaining to sex?"

Self-Love Exercise: Find different things that help turn your BFF on. Is a pair of heels? A skirt with no panties? Is it that scrumptious person at the local coffee shop that you flirt with on a daily basis? Pay attention to what makes her swell up with joy and do more of that! Don't forget to say hello to her too!

Planner: Plan a sexy stay at home date for yourself or for you and your partner.

Schedule some time for reflecting on Day 5 & 6. This time can be added to your bedtime routine with a cup of hot tea if you desire.

Reflection days are just as important as activity days. These days are added to the 8-week workbook to allow you time to reflect on your own without the exercises. It is important to journal during these days.

Congratulations Goddess, You've Completed Week 3!

You've also completed part 1 of the Sex part of the Goddess Workbook.

❀ Week Four

Welcome to! This week we are going to explore orgasms and the journey of sexual pleasure. I hope you are excited Goddess because the good news is you don't need to have a partner to participate in this week's exercises.

This week's exercises are built for you to become more sexually intimate with yourself and this includes understanding your sexual pleasure. For some Goddesses, these activities can be a little bit far out so please be gentle with yourself.

Day 1 Exercise 1: It's time to think of all the ways you have reached climax. In the spaces below write down the ways you or your partner helped you reach climax. Please just focus on the act that allowed you to arrive to climax for example: Make out session led to my first orgasm of the night.

1. _____
2. _____
3. _____
4. _____
5. _____
6. _____
7. _____

For this section of the exercise, please write down more specific details you can remember when you reached climax. For example: I remember during the make out session there were candles lit and I felt relaxed.

1. _____

2. _____

3. _____

4. _____

5. _____

6. _____

7. _____

Journal: In today's exercise you explored situations that helped you climax. For this journal entry let's expand on other ways that you can reach climax. These ways can be things you haven't tried, only tried once, or want to try again.

This is important to know this about yourself and understand that orgasms can sometimes not be reached. This is perfectly normal! You are studying your context. Context: meaning what you need to FEEL before and during a yummy session to reach climax.

Self-Love: Write a list of phrases that someone has said to you that turned you on and create affirmations from that list. For example: "I love the way your skin feels, so soft" to "I love the way my skin feels, so soft."

Planner: Plan something "naughty" this week. Like buying a sex toy or wear a long sexy skirt with no panties. Whatever you feel comfortable doing, plan for it and prepare for it, especially if it includes someone else.

Day 2 Exercise 1: In this exercise, I want you to think of a bad sexual experience you had. Think about why it was awful. Were you not into it? Did you not want to have sex but did it anyway? Did the person finish too soon, and you were left lying there? Anything you would like to explore as an awful sexual experience please write it (them) below. *Please be aware of any feelings you are feeling as you write this (these) experience(s).

Journal: Today's journal entry is about today's exercise. Make note of any feelings that come up during this exercise, good or bad. Take notice if this experience has stopped or delayed your sexual growth? Notice if it made you not want to try new things? Or if it pushed you into risky behaviors outside of sex? Write down as much or as little as you like and remember to be gentle with yourself.

Self-Love: Please take note of what you wrote down for your exercise. If you've experienced sexual trauma, please do not hesitate to seek assistance from a licensed therapist. They can help you heal from the sexual trauma while you are being coached.

Planner: Make plans to speak with someone if you have experienced sexual trauma. Or if you are already speaking to someone, make plans to love yourself this week. Example: One of the reflection days can be used as a day of forgiveness, release, and love. This is a practice, planning just one day will not heal all of your heart right away. You must continue to plan for days of forgiveness.

Day 3 Exercise 1: What are you seeking? Are you seeking more sex or more pleasurable fulfilling sex? To achieve more pleasurable fulfilling sex, you must dive a little deeper. Forget about the things your parents, school, and our friends have told us what sex should be like and start to tap in what sex should be like to you! In this section, you will write down ways for you to achieve a more pleasurable fulfilling sexual experience.

For example: I have a gentleman caller who I am not committed to. He comes over maybe twice a week and I love preparing for his arrival. I love knowing that I am not attached to someone beyond just sexual pleasures. I don't have to cook for him, clean for him, and I believe that makes our visits so much more fun & fulfilling!

As women, we are taught we MUST be in a loving committed relationship with our significant other to have fulfilling sex. As you can see from the example above, that is not entirely true. So feel free to allow your desires to fly!

_____

_____

_____

_____

_____

_____

_____

_____

_____

_____

_____

_____

_____

Journal: Today's entry will focus on what's been holding you back from sexual pleasure or any pleasurable experience? In today's exercise, did you write down your vision of a pleasurable fulfilling sexual experience or did you write down a past experience that you perceived as pleasurable and fulfilling? Either way, what is stopping you from feeling pleasure all of the time (or even just most of it)? Is it the way you perceive pleasure? Is it only in a sexual experience? Does society play a role in your perception? Does your past play a role in your perception?

Self-Love: Indulge in a simple pleasure today. Is it a strawberry ice cream cone? Is it going to bed with freshly shaved legs? Find a couple of your simple pleasures and indulge in them. Savor the moment. Smile. Feel aroused. Joyous.

Planner: Plan to indulge in a bigger pleasure this week. Is it getting your hair down? Does that make you feel like a Goddess? Or going to a wine tasting? Only you know what pleases you! So, let's plan for pleasure!

Day 4 Exercise 1: Taking responsibility for our own sexual pleasure. We often believe that the other person should know exactly what to do, where to go, how long to last, etc. without us showing them (demonstrating how you want to be touched), guiding them (taking their hand and showing them where you want to be touched), or communicating deeply with them (Outside of the act of having sex in a conversation). We are unaware of how much in control we are when it comes to sexual pleasure and we undoubtably leave ourselves unsatisfied.

This exercise is aimed to help that. Write down ways that you can take back control of your sexual pleasure. Is it to self-please more so you can know your hot spots, fantasies, etc. better? Or is it communicating, guiding, etc.?

1. _____

2. _____

3. _____

4. _____

5. _____

6. _____

7. _____

8. _____

9. _____

10. _____

Journal: Today's was about taking back control of your sexual pleasure. It is not an easy process. There are often underlying challenges that we are not aware of that hold us back. In today's journal entry we are going to write about 'NO.' Who told you no? For example: No, I can't try oral sex because my mother said good girls don't do that. I wanted to be a respectable woman, so I don't give my partner oral sex.

The no can come from anywhere, friends, family, religion, society. Explore who told you no when it comes to your sexual pleasure and write down if it has stopped or slowed down your sexual growth. *Please take note of how you are feeling. The no's can run very deep. So be gentle with yourself.

Self-Love: Relax. Easier said than done. However, after a deep dive the past couple of days, you want to relax and do something that makes you laugh, dance, sing, or just plain happy!

Planner: Do something fun! Plan on having some adult fun this week!

Schedule some time for reflecting on Day 5 & 6. This time can be added to your bedtime routine with a cup of hot tea if you desire.

Reflection days are just as important as activity days. These days are added to the 8-week workbook to allow you time to reflect on your own without the exercises. It is important to journal during these days.

Congratulations Goddess, You've Completed Week 4!
You've also completed part 2 of the Sex part of the Goddess Workbook.

❀Week Five

Congratulations Goddess, you are half-way through the 8-week workbook! You should be absolutely proud of yourself! So far in this workbook you have discovered and faced fears, loved on your body, learned how to breathe and self-care...whoa! You have done a lot! Now, it is time for us to move on to the second half of the Goddess Workbook.

Sex is just one part of pleasure. Sensuality takes pleasure out of the bedroom and into your everyday life. There are things we hurry through that we need to take the time to enjoy. These two weeks will help you take some time to explore your sensuality! Enjoy!

Day 1 Exercise 1: Special occasions don't come as often as they should, thank goodness you are a Goddess, and every day is a special occasion! In this exercise you are to prepare your home in the most delightful and romantic way as if you are getting ready to host a special occasion (ex: partner's birthday, anniversary, a congratulations celebration). If you are married, then prepare for two. If you are single, prepare for one.

You are to prepare for a romantic night at home. Use whatever makes YOU feel sensual and elegant. The point of this exercise is to enjoy all of the stages of the night. From preparation to the finish project. Keep in mind that you are celebrating YOU! Use the space below to write out ideas or items that you need to gather.

_____

_____

_____

_____

_____

_____

_____

_____

_____

_____

_____

_____

_____

_____

In today's exercise you were asked to prepare your home romantically, like it was a special occasion. In this entry, please write down how this makes you feel? Did you savor the moment? Was it difficult for you to focus in the moment? Celebrating ourselves is not something we are taught. Please ask yourself if you felt selfish. Especially, if you are married or have a significant other. Even though you were sharing a meal with them, did you feel self-centered that you were celebrating YOU?

Sensuality Self-Care: Never stop celebrating yourself! Allow yourself to sit in a comfortable and quiet place and focus on your breathing. This is the time to envision yourself being celebrated. Focus on the feelings of being happy, appreciated, joyous, etc. Remember, you are worthy of celebration.

Planner: Plan another celebration dinner at least once a month. Allow yourself to have luxuries that you don't often buy during this time. It could be food, flowers, a new piece of jewelry…anything! You are a Goddess, and you should celebrate you!

Day 2 Exercise 1: Goddess Bath. Ever heard of Queens and Goddess bathing luxuriously? Well, this is your time to treat yourself to a Goddess Bath. This is the time where you treat yourself like the Goddess that you are to some self-care & self-love time.

Prepare a bath with flower petals, oils, etc. Relax with candles, music, and your favorite drink. Be in the moment. Bathe every part of your beautiful body. Notice how your skin looks in the candlelight, how the steam rolls off of your legs etc.

Use the space below to write down anything you may need for your Goddess bath:

_____

_____

_____

_____

_____

_____

_____

_____

_____

_____

_____

_____

_____

_____

_____

_____

_____

_____

Bathing or showering tends to be a "to do" thing not something that we allow to be sensual. Today's entry is a reflection about how you felt about preparing and during the bath.

Did you feel silly? Or did you feel like a Goddess preparing her luxurious bathing experience? Whatever you feel is perfect for you.

Sensuality Self-Care: You already bathed like a Goddess, so your Sensuality Self-Care is covered for the day.

Planner: Plan to take a Goddess bath at least once a month. You can also plan to prepare Goddess baths on tough & stressful days. Scheduling a luxurious bath gives you something to look forward to.

Day 3 Exercise 1: Try on a new life! When was the last time you dreamed? When was the last time you envisioned yourself as the beautiful Goddess that you are strolling down the street and all adoring eyes were on you because of your light and sensuality?

Today's exercise is to try on a dress or an outfit that you would never on any other day. Or test drive that luxury car or take that open house tour. The point is not to buy anything, it's the feeling of being around beautiful things. It's knowing you deserve anything you desire. So, dress to impress yourself & enter every room today as if you are bursting with love and light.

Write down five things that you thought you would never have, because of how expensive or how nice you it was, that you now have:

1. _____

2. _____

3. _____

4. _____

5. _____

6. _____

7. _____

A woman's desires light her up and turn her on! Today you were asked to "try on" your desires. You didn't have to buy anything that you desired today (if you did and you are absolutely in love with it...good for you!) In today's journal entry write down how you felt. Did you feel powerful, sexy, important? Did you feel your desires are more in your reach? Were you turned on sexually when you saw yourself in the mirror wearing that sexy dress? Or did you feel like you could ask your honey for as many favors as you liked wearing a pair of booty hugging jeans?

Sensuality Self-Care: Fix yourself or buy yourself your favorite dish and savor every bite. Chew slowly. Allow the flavors to caress your tongue. Moan if you feel like moaning. This is the time to take a moment for yourself and indulge!

Planner: If you found a piece of luxury during today's exercise that you absolutely desire, plan to obtain it! You deserve everything you desire! Give yourself enough time to reach said desire. For example: A house may take longer than a car so allow 6 months to a year to obtain a house that you desire depending on where you are at now. Research timelines and ask a real-estate agent.

Day 4 Exercise 1: Let Sensuality Flow through you! Now you have some idea of what turns you on. It is important to know how to use that particular energy. Just because you are turned on doesn't mean you always have to have sex and self-please. It's also amazing to allow sensual feelings to flow through your body. We are women and we create! Sensuality helps us create wonderful things!

Today, you are to allow yourself to be sensually turned on and create something wonderful!

Create movement (do yoga or dance). Create a space (reorganize your room add or take away). Create art (paint or mold something out of clay). What you can create is limitless! Use the sensual energy to create something amazing.

Journal: Did today's exercise seem a little different or awkward? Have you allowed yourself to be turned on and used that energy to create with? Was this your first time? Today journal entry, write down your experience today. What did you create? How did it feel creating it? Sensual energy can be used for more than just sex.

Sensuality Self-Care: Treat yourself to a little erotica. Listen or read an erotic story. Allow your imagination to run wild!

Planner: If you find a yoga practice, creative hobby, or anything that you enjoyed during this exercise, plan to do it again!

Reflection days are just as important as activity days. These days are added to the 8-week workbook to allow you time to reflect on your own without the exercises. It is important to journal during these days.

Congratulations Goddess, You've Completed Week 5!

You've also completed part 1 of the Sensuality part of Goddess Workbook.

❧ Week Six

It is important to enjoy your own company. We are taught to rush through life, have someone always there, and that being alone & pleasing oneself is wrong and selfish. Well, I am here to tell you Goddess, it is neither wrong nor selfish to be alone or pleasing to yourself! This week is about slowing down, taking time for pure pleasure, demanding nothing less, and to not feeling lonely when you're alone.

Day 1 Exercise 1: What was told to you? As a woman, we are told that we need to get married by a certain age, have children by a certain age, and so forth. The details are different with every woman. So, in this exercise, you are to write down common phrases you were told growing up and or now, about how you are "supposed" to be when it comes to being a woman. Example: My mother told me a good wife means to allow the man to make all of the financial decisions.

Did these statements above impact your views on how you approach sensuality? Example: "Because I allowed my husband to make all of the financial decisions, I do not feel in control of what I want to buy. I feel like a little kid when I want to buy a piece of lingerie or a toy because I have to ask permission. So, I just avoid those types of desires altogether. I guess it has impacted my sensuality in a negative way. I do not feel like a sensual grown woman, I feel like a little girl".

_____

_____

_____

_____

_____

_____

_____

_____

_____

_____

_____

_____

Journal: Today you had to remember phrases that helped mold your views about being a woman, or what a woman should be. Sensuality is more than just sexual intercourse; however, we do not explore such things due to how we "should" act. For today's journal entry, let's explore who you would be if you never heard any of those phrases. Would you buy that popsicle and eat it in public without hesitation? Would you get a sexy hair style and wear it to the family reunion? Who would you be if you NEVER heard any of these limiting beliefs?

Sensuality Self-Care: Look at yourself in the mirror and imagine all of the beautiful body parts you want to kiss. Notice your breathing, your joy, imagine what each body part being kissed feels the best. Allow your imagination to run wild!

Planner: Think of an activity you wouldn't do before this journey and plan to do it! Like taking a pole dancing class or going to a naked yoga class. Choose something bold. And if you don't like it after you tried it...explore the reasons why this activity did not bring you joy and try something else. *This doesn't have to be done by the end of this week.

Day 2 Exercise 1: In this exercise you are to write activities that you believe you need someone to do them with and then write down the ways you can do these activities on your own.

Activities that I believe I need a partner:

1. _____
   _____
   _____

2. _____
   _____
   _____

3. _____
   _____
   _____

4. _____
   _____
   _____

5. _____
   _____

How I can enjoy these activities without a partner:

1. _____
   _____
   _____

2. _____
   _____
   _____

3. _____
   _____
   _____

4. _____
   _____
   _____

5. _____
   _____

Journal: Fantasize about a vacation you would love to take by yourself. Imagine the people you would meet, the places you would go to eat, and what type of hotel room you would stay in, etc. This is your time to explore who you are when it comes to travel and vacation by yourself. Please include some fears and concerns in this fantasy so you can write down ways to help overcome them.

Sensuality Self-Care: Turn up the music in your car or in your bedroom and dance! Sing! Be Silly! Allow the music to flow through you and play whatever you are feeling at the time. The only rule is…do this when no one is around.

Planner: Plan an overnight stay by yourself somewhere fun and sensual to you. It can be as simple as staying in a hotel with a huge bathtub in your own town! The point is, getting over the fear of being by yourself and enjoying your own company. *This doesn't have to be planned for the same week.

Day 3 Exercise 1: Early in this workbook we explored our bodies with touch. We are going to do this again but from a different approach. Select your favorite lotion, oil, shea butter, etc. and start to slowly place it on your skin. Make mental notes of what parts soak in the moisture quickly, what needs more moisture, and what areas of your skin glows. Don't say anything negative about your skin or body part. Just observe. Observe the pressure you use on different body parts…

This exercise is to help you be present with your body. The way you see your body now may be different than how you've seen it earlier in this workbook. We must constantly reintroduce ourselves to ourselves in the most loving way possible. You can put on some meditation music if you would like.

Journal: In this journal entry, you are to write down what views changed when it comes to your body. Remember how you used to feel about your body and your sensuality before the program started versus now. Write down at least 5 things that have changed. Please also include your emotions in this journal entry.

Sensuality Self-Care: Your self-loving massage was your self-care for the day! Good job!

Planner: Give yourself a break to breathe! Yes, we are circling back to breathing. Taking a moment to breathe and regroup is always important.

*This week has extra reflection days! So, plan some time to breathe during those extra days!

This weekday 4, 5, 6, & 7 are all reflection days! The last two weeks are to help you plan to put what you have learned into practice with a little guidance. Enjoy!

❀ Week Seven

Week 1: Write out a plan of action! Plan a full week by your beautiful self! Use the space below to list activities, breathing methods, and self-care events that you would like to try. Next, place them in your planner for the week! (Try not to overdo it. Having small activities during the week is best).

_____

_____

_____

_____

_____

_____

_____

_____

_____

_____

_____

_____

_____

_____

- Use the tools you have learned in the previous weeks!

- Look at problems as opportunities to grow!

- Create personalized affirmations!

A safe space for thoughts like doubts, fears, etc. It is important to be gentle with yourself:

Peace, Sex, *and Sensuality*

Week 2: Write out a plan of action but add one thing you haven't done before! Plan another full week by your beautiful self! (Remember: Practice makes progress!) Use the space below to list activities, breathing methods, and self-care events that you would like to try. Next, place them in your planner for the week! (Try not to overdo it. Having small activities during the week is best).

_____
_____
_____
_____
_____
_____
_____
_____
_____
_____
_____
_____
_____
_____

- Use the tools you have learned in the previous weeks!

- Look at problems/challenges as opportunities to grow!

- Create personalized affirmations!

A safe space for thoughts like doubts, fears, etc. It is important to be gentle with yourself:

_____
_____
_____
_____

Congratulations Goddess! You have completed the workbook! Just because the workbook is completed doesn't mean you are...YOU keep growing.

- Continue to make time for your peace every day. Finding your peace will help you focus, put you in a better mood to make better and healthier decisions for yourself. *Honor the not-so-great feelings as well! These feelings are a part of you. Don't push them aside because you believe you need to be happy and peaceful all of the time.
- Continue to explore your sexual side! Find different ways to climax, fantasize, heal from sexual trauma (if it applies to you), communicate your desires in the bedroom etc.
- Continue to find sensuality in everything! Do things that light you up and bring you joy. Follow your BFF's advice, you know the one we carry around with us every day...listen to her.
- Continue to put yourself first. It is not selfish! You need to be healthy and whole to provide and nurture for anyone else.

And above all of this:

Remember YOU are a Goddess!

Self-Evaluation

Welcome back Goddess, I am so excited to see you have completed this amazing journey!

Now it is time to see if your mindset has shifted. This self-evaluation will help you see where you stand after you have completed the workbook exercises. Please fill out and answer the questions listed below. Remember, there are no right or wrong answers, just honest ones! After you have completed the evaluation compare it to your first one eight weeks ago and rejoice in how much you have grown!

On a scale from 1 to 10, with 1 being the lowest (very poor) to 10 being the highest (excellent), please answer the following questions. Note: Some questions may ask you to explain your answer.

1. What level would you rate your self-confidence?
    a. 1 2 3 4 5 6 7 8 9 10
2. What would help you increase your self-confidence?

    _____

    _____

    _____

3. What level would you rate your self-care routine?
    a. 1 2 3 4 5 6 7 8 9 10
4. What level would you rate your sex life?
    a. 1 2 3 4 5 6 7 8 9 10
5. Overall, what level would you rate your happiness?
    a. 1 2 3 4 5 6 7 8 9 10
    b. Please explain your answer.

    _____

    _____

    _____

6. What level would you rate your love life?
    a. 1 2 3 4 5 6 7 8 9 10
7. How well can you communicate your desires and wants to

your partner or anyone else in your life?

   a. 1 2 3 4 5 6 7 8 9 10

8. Is there anyone you can NOT express desires and wants to? Y or N

   a. Please explain your answer.

_____

_____

_____

Please answer yes or no to the following questions:

1. Do you feel more comfortable with your body now? Y or N
2. Do you feel you are normal when it comes to sex? Y or N
3. Do you still compare yourself in a negative way to models or other women? Y or N
4. Do you still find it difficult to stay on track when it comes to taking care of yourself? Y or N
5. (Parent or Caregivers Only) Do you still find it difficult to feel and/or look sexy while being a parent or a caregiver? Y or N

Please answer the following questions:

1. Are you still experiencing things now that you did not want to experience before? Y or N
2. How do you feel on a daily basis?

_____

_____

_____

_____

3. What wonderful things are happening for you now?

_____

_____

_____

www.ingramcontent.com/pod-product-compliance
Lightning Source LLC
Chambersburg PA
CBHW020921140626
46545CB00015B/1105